What Can I...
Smell

Sue Barraclough

Raintree

Chicago, Illinois

CANCEL

© 2005 Raintree
an imprint of Capstone Global Library, LLC
Chicago, Illinois
Customer Service 888-363-4266
Visit our website at www.raintreelibrary.com

Printed and bound by South China Printing Company.
15 14 13 12 11
10 9 8 7 6 5

Library of Congress Cataloging-in-Publication Data:
Barraclough, Sue.
  What can I smell? / Sue Barraclough.
     p. cm. -- (What can I?)
  Includes index.
  ISBN 1-4109-2164-6 (library binding-hardcover) -- ISBN 1-4109-2170-0
(pbk.) ISBN 978-1-4109-2164-2 (library binding-hardcover) -- ISBN 978-1-4109-2170-3 (pbk.)
 1. Smell--Juvenile literature. I. Title: Smell?. II. Title. III.
Series: Barraclough, Sue. What can I?
  QP458.B36 2005
  612.8'6--dc22

                    2004026301

Acknowledgments
The Publishers would like to thank the following for permission to reproduce photographs:
Corbis p.**13** bottom; Corbis p.**17** inset (Craig Aurness), **13** top (George Shelley), **20** (Kelly-Mooney Photography); Getty Images / ThinkStock pp.**22-23**; Getty Images / PhotoDisc pp.**10**, **13** right, **21** top; Harcourt Education pp.**14-15** (Peter Evans Photography), **4-5**, **6**, **7**, **8**, **9**, **12**, **15** inset, **16-17** (Tudor Photography); Powerstock pp.**11**, **18**; Robert Harding Picture Library p.**19**; Zefa / Masterfile p.**21** right and bottom.

Cover photograph reproduced with permission of Harcourt Education Ltd. / Trevor Clifford.

Every effort has been made to contact copyright holders of any material reproduced in this book. Any omissions will be rectified in subsequent printings if notice is given to the publishers.

Some words are shown in bold, **like this**. You can find out what they mean by looking in the glossary on page 24.

2

Contents

Breakfast Smells

Breakfast is ready. Warm toast smells good.

What is your favorite breakfast smell?

Clean and Fresh

Soap and toothpaste smell fresh and clean.

Clean socks smell nice.
How do dirty socks smell?

Favorite Smells

This rabbit likes the smell of carrots. Do you?

Sniff, sniff!

Flowers

Butterflies and bees like flowers that smell sweet.

bzzzzzz!

Nice Smells

Some **perfumes** smell sweet like flowers.

Do you like the
smell of these
things?

The smell is very strong.

Smells Delicious!

Bakeries sell fresh cakes, cookies, pies, and bread.

Park Smells

Garbage cans are stinky!

18

bzzzzzz!

What do you see here that might smell good?

19

Animal Noses

These goats smell food!

Look at these different animal noses.

Bedtime

After a warm bath, all fresh and clean, it's time for bed.

Goodnight, and sweet dreams!

Glossary

garbage can   place to put trash
perfume   nice-smelling liquid

Index

Notes for Adults

Books in the *What Can I...* series encourage children to use their senses to actively explore the world around them.

Additional Information
A sniff carries air in through the nose via the nostrils into an area called the nasal cavity. The top of the nasal cavity has millions of tiny hairy cells that can detect different odors. These cells then send information to the brain for processing.

Follow-up activities
• Cooking and baking activities, a walk in the park, or a shopping trip are good ways to focus on and explore different smells. Encourage children to describe a smell they can identify. Ask them if the smell reminds them of anything or to compare it to other smells.